Conformed to the Image of God's Son

Roger London

*"We know that in everything God works for good
with those who love Him, who are called according
to His purpose. For those whom He foreknew
He also predestined to be conformed to the image
of His Son, in order that He might be the first-born
among many brethren. And those whom He
predestined He also called; and those whom
He called He also justified; and those whom
He justified He also glorified"*
(Romans 8:28-30)

Conformed to the Image of God's Son

First published in Great Britain in 2014 by
Much Fruit Publishing
muchfruitpublishing@gmail.com

A catalogue record for this book is
available from the British Library

ISBN 978-0-9928955-0-1

Printed and bound in Uganda by
Mentart Design, Kampala

Cover design by **Roopop Design**

Conformed to the Image of God's Son

Contents

Foreword

Roger London – teacher, brother, friend – is, under God, a gift from the West to the Church today in these challenging times we are living in. Roger has put us in debt by giving us this interesting easy-to-read book.

Jesus is soon coming again, according to the promise in the Word of God, the Bible. Although many people, especially those from the West, including some Christians, will have none of this, it will not take away the imminence of His return. In *Conformed to the Image of God's Son,* Roger shares with us, in a simple straightforward way, what the Church must do to be ready for when Jesus will come.

I have been privileged to go on missions with Roger across many nations in Africa. We have ministered together, travelled on bumpy, rough roads, together, and eaten the same food, including *njara* (an Ethiopian delicacy).So, as I was reading this book, it was as if Roger was standing there ministering to me live. I could almost see his expressions and sweat running down his face under the punishing heat of Africa. This is the advantage a person has who reads a book written by an author he has heard ministering before. As you go through *Conformed to the Image of God's Son,* let Roger minister to you. Do not be in a hurry to finish the book as if you were timed. Read it thoughtfully and prayerfully, with your Bible by your side, looking at all the quotations mentioned therein and confirm for yourself that what is being said is the truth. Be like the saints from Berea mentioned in Acts 17:11-12:

"The people of Berea were more open-minded than those in Thessalonica, and they listened eagerly to Paul's message. They searched the Scriptures day after day to see if Paul and Silas were teaching the truth."

In many churches worldwide Christians are satisfied by just having a born again experience, and their leaders, in most cases, do not know better. No true believer can dispute the fact that being born again is a wonderful and necessary experience. But is that all there is for us in salvation? What did God have in mind when He sent His beloved Son to come and die for us? In *Conformed to the Image of God's Son* you will discover that God wants all of His children to be conformed to the image of His Son Jesus. You will be taken through a wonderful process of spiritual transformation step by step. This is a must read - I both urge and encourage you to read this book.

My prayer is that by reading this book your life will be so transformed and then, through you, that of your family and friends also.

God bless you!

Bishop Laban Mbabazi
(Christ's Co-workers Church, Uganda, and Watchmen International African Executive Team Member)

Introduction

In many Ugandan Pentecostal churches, believers are used to being put on the spot following the adult Sunday School preaching on a Sunday morning – "So, you there, what have you learned from today's message?" The one addressed would then stand to his or her feet and either remain silent, offer a few confused sentences, or, as was often the case, say something quite relevant to what had been preached. Generally, in my visits to local churches in Uganda, I will not be so direct, being British, but often I still like to engage the congregation with questions during the delivery of my teaching. Doing this during the message rather than at the end helps me to see just how much of the message is clearly understood rather than trying to get the believers to repeat something I have already said. On a few occasions, in different churches, I have asked the following question, "What is the gospel?" At first, on each occasion the question was met with a deathly silence. So I added to the original question, "The gospel means 'good news' – so what is the good news contained in the Bible?" The silence continued for a while and then a few thoughts began to be offered by different congregational members. "God loves us" was one such answer; another was "Jesus died for the whole World"; a third was "Jesus forgives us for our sin"; a fourth was "One day we will meet Jesus in heaven". I think if I were to ask the same question in every church I visit in Africa the answers would probably be very similar – basic gospel truths which every believer should know, often from childhood.

But what about the West, where generally believers receive much more Bible teaching? What if I were to ask the same questions to believers in local churches there? Would the answers be roughly the same? Perhaps the answers would be a little more detailed as we are more used to a learning style prompted by questions, rather than learning by rote. However, I believe the answers would not be too different.

The question which arises in my mind at this juncture is – 'What is the gospel that has been taught in our churches for so many years?' Is it not something like: God loves us; we have all sinned and fallen short of His plan and will for our lives; the consequences of this are that we will die and end up going to Hell; but God, in his love, has provided a solution, sending His own Son to earth to live among us and then to die in our place, taking the punishment for our sins; if we receive Christ as our Saviour, then God will forgive us, give us new life and offer us a place in heaven with Him when we die. This summary might appear a little simplistic but nevertheless would be roughly how most believers might express in words what the gospel is. Often these truths have been impressed on us from an early age supported by a few clear pointers in well-used gospel tracts and booklets

Of course, the above points all represent aspects of the wonderful gospel which we find within the pages of God's Word, but they are only a part. In fact they fall well short of the fullness of the gospel, of God's 'good news' for each and every one of us. To have fully grasped the gospel is to have understood what is in the heart and mind of God for you and me – what is His end goal for us. To understand God's great plan for us will help us to understand the purpose of much of the exhortational teaching in the New Testament as to how we should be living as believers in and followers of Jesus Christ.

Please read on and I believe the pieces of the gospel jig-saw will come together for you in a way that you may never have seen before – hopefully the huge centre-piece of the jigsaw will be placed into your hand and then the Word of God will come alive to you in a new and dynamic way. Many pieces of the jigsaw which previously didn't appear to fit will hopefully now slot into place effortlessly.

Finally, you will find within this book many scriptures written out for you. I don't apologise for that. I am a firm believer in the power of the Word of God to speak for itself. We are living in a day and age, when many church sermons are based on good morals and good ideas rather than on the truth as it is revealed in God's Word. Few preachers and teachers actually encourage their congregations to bring their Bibles to church, and few believers get the opportunity to look up scriptures during the delivery of sermons because the Word of God is often only casually referred to. Please take time to carefully read the scriptures, go to the Bible, read around the scriptures contained in this book in order to understand the context of what is being said. Use a concordance or internet search tool such as www.biblegateway.com to search God's Word for other examples of scriptures which may support or confirm what is being said. As the advertisement for yellow pages used to say – 'Let your fingers do the walking'.

Roger London

Destined to be just like Jesus

In Paul's letter to the Romans, he declares in chapter one, as the theme of his written message, that he is not ashamed of the gospel, for it is the power of God for salvation to everyone who has faith (Romans 1:16). That statement is really like a title for Paul's letter – he then proceeds to unpack the 'good news', and its implications for each and every one of us, over sixteen wonderful chapters.

Paul's unpacking of the gospel in Romans is rather like climbing a mountain with an end goal of arriving at the peak in order to take in the glorious panorama laid out before you – for those of you who delight in climbing hills and mountains you will know how breathtakingly beautiful arriving at the peak can be. I remember one such experience on the Island of Madeira, off the West African Coast, when turning a corner near the summit of Pico do Arieiro, my wife, Glenys, and I were suddenly confronted by the spectacle of seeing huge swathes of puffy white cloud lying beneath us, just as if we were flying in an aeroplane, but, instead, we were standing still, awed by what lay beneath us. Paul's gospel panorama is seen in all its glory in the wonderful verses of chapter eight of his letter where he reaches the peak of his explanation of the gospel. But how do you pick out the precise peak of the gospel in that wonderful chapter – it's simply full of breath-taking statements – no condemnation for those who are in Christ Jesus, led by the Spirit of God, sons of God, children of God, heirs of God, joint heirs with Christ, destined for incomparable glory, waiting for adoption as sons, nothing can separate us from God's love, more than conquerors – it's as if you are circumnavigating a broad peak plateau, as with Table Mountain overlooking Cape Town, South Africa, declaring at different points, "Well, this must be the high point", only to be surprised by yet more glorious views.

However there's one short sentence that surpasses all the others in chapter eight, upon which all the others hang, and it is found in verse 29 – a verse which is often overlooked in the light of all the other better known verses from that chapter:
"For those whom He foreknew he also predestined to be conformed to the image of His Son, in order that He might be the first-born among many brethren."

The height or goal of the gospel, the end purpose in God's heart and mind for you and me, is that we will be fashioned and shaped by Him until we conform exactly to the image of Jesus, His Son. I often teach that if God's purposes for me were just forgiveness of sins and an eternal home in heaven, then that would be totally amazing because, in reality, I deserve absolutely nothing but God's judgement – and that applies to each and every one of us. "As long as I make it to heaven, God can put me in a small corner somewhere – even that would be truly amazing" would be my sentiment. However, God's eternal plan for us far surpassesall our normal summaries of the 'good news' and also far exceeds any of our expectations – it is nothing less than conformity to the image of Jesus Himself!

Of course, nothing of God's ultimate plan could ever have been achieved without the sacrifice of God's Son on the cross, paving the way for every step of salvation from new birth to total transformation into the likeness of Jesus.

The Greek word *'summorphous'* translated as *'conformed'* in Romans 8:29, literally means 'of the same form or appearance'. Our eternal destiny is that we will share the same form or appearance as Jesus Himself.

In his letter to the Philippians, Paul uses the same Greek word, writing:
"But our commonwealth is in heaven, and from it we await a Saviour, the Lord Jesus Christ, who will change our lowly body *to be like* His glorious body" (Philippians 3:20-21).

Again, in his first letter to the Corinthian church, Paul, in writing about the nature of the resurrection body that all true believers will receive on Christ's return, states:
"Just as we have borne the image of the man of dust, we shall also bear the image of the man of heaven" (1 Corinthians 15:49).
The Greek word *'eikona'*, translated as *'image'* in this scripture, literally means *'exact likeness'*.

This amazing truth is further confirmed to us in John's first letter when he writes:
"Beloved, we are God's children now; it does not yet appear what we shall be, but we know that when He appears we shall *be like* (Greek: *'homoio'* = made like, resemble) Him, for we shall see Him as He is" (1 John 3:2).

This is nothing short of staggering, mind-blowing and almost blasphemous but, nevertheless, true: it is God's plan for you and me to be clothed with a new body that resembles that of the risen, exalted and glorified Jesus Himself!

Paul goes on to write in Romans 8:29 that the result of being conformed to the image of God's Son is that Jesus will be the first-born among many brothers. Although Jesus will ever remain unique as the eternal Son of God, in another sense he will have many that resemble Him – like brothers and sisters!
A key question we now need to ask is 'When does this transformation into the likeness of Jesus begin?' I think the popular understanding of believers would be that the transformation takes place upon the return of Jesus, for, as both Paul and John write, it is when we see Him that we shall be like Him. Paul writes in 1 Corinthians 15:51-52:
"Lo! I tell you a mystery. We shall not all sleep, but we shall all be changed, in a moment, in the twinkling of an eye, at the last trumpet."
However, I want to suggest that this is only part of the truth – the 'icing on the cake' if you like, but when the full truth is fully grasped, it causes so much of the New Testament teaching on the need for spiritual transformation to fall into place. Transformation into the likeness of Jesus actually begins at the point of regeneration, or new birth, and continues throughout our lives to the point when, meeting Jesus, on His return, the transformation is completed.

John states in his letter that, for the one who is truly born of God, God's seed (Greek: 'sperma' = seed, semen) dwells within him (1 John 3:9). Peter's first letter sheds further light on this by stating that we have been born anew of imperishable seed (Greek: '*sporos*' = spore, seed, 1 Peter 1:23). Clearly, these scriptures indicate that, at the point of new birth, God injects his reproductive seed into a person, unseen to the natural eye and investigation, but, nevertheless, truly implanted into the heart of a man or woman. Now what does this seed represent? It is nothing short of an implanting of God's very life and nature into us. A tiny element of what God is in essence, an exact reproduction of His glorious nature, is planted into our hearts in seed form. Now, just as with human reproduction, where, in this case, it is both the seed of a man and a woman that unites to produce a brand new created being, so with spiritual conception (although spiritual conception and spiritual birth are one and the same in this illustration) the seed begins to grow and multiply, gradually taking shape. The glorious seed begins to grow and to take on a glorious form - unseen to the natural eye, but clearly seen and recognised by God Himself, and one day, to also be seen by us, in all its glory. I remember seeing a fast forward of the development that takes place within a woman's womb, from the tiny fertilised human seed to a fully grown baby – I was awestruck by the miracle taking place before my eyes. Well, spiritually speaking a similar miracle is taking place within us as we are being changed into the likeness of Jesus Himself.

But how can we be sure that this is not just wishful thinking? Well, take a look at Paul's second letter to the Corinthian church. In chapter three he states:
"And we all, with unveiled face, beholding (or reflecting) the glory of the Lord, are being changed into His likeness from

one degree of glory to another; for this comes from the Lord who is the Spirit" (2 Corinthians 3:18).

Transformation into the likeness of Jesus is a 'here and now' activity of the Spirit of God in the lives of believers, not just a future transformation that takes place on Jesus' return. Being transformed into the exact form and appearance of Jesus begins at the moment of spiritual new birth and continues throughout our spiritual lives here on earth until the point, when, meeting Jesus face to face, that transformation is completed.

When Jesus returns and we are caught up to meet him in the air, our earthly body, whether we are physically dead or alive at that moment, is no longer needed. Paul describes this earthly body as being like a clay pot, which hides the forming of the glory of God within us from our eyes (2 Corinthians 4:7). At that moment the full glory of God's nature within us, which he has been fashioning and growing day by day, will be seen by all, radiating through the new heavenly body given at that precise moment.

What I have been describing is summed up by the New Testament word 'glorification' (to be glorified, transformed into the likeness of Jesus Himself) – which is both a present and future work of the Spirit in our lives and we shall later see that glorification is fully linked to another New Testament word 'sanctification' (to be set apart as holy and for holy use).

Salvation – a 'One-off' Event or a Process?

In the light of the glorious spiritual transformation described in the previous chapter it is clear that salvation is not a 'one-off event', as viewed by many, but rather a process that begins at new birth and continues until the day we meet Jesus. This truth is well supported within the New Testament:
In his letter to the Ephesians Paul writes:
"By grace you *have been* saved" (Ephesians 2:5).
However, when addressing the Corinthian church, Paul speaks of the message of the cross as being the power of God "to us who are *being* saved (1 Corinthians 1:18).
Finally, in the Olivet discourse in Matthew's Gospel, Jesus declares:
"He who endures to the end *will be* saved" (Matthew 24:13).

In summary then, we can state, as believers in Jesus Christ, that we have been saved (we have come to a point of regeneration, where we have been justified – that is, declared righteous in God's sight), we are being saved (a process of spiritual transformation has begun and is continuing in our lives – this is sanctification, accompanied by glorification), and we will be saved (if we continue in the process of spiritual transformation and hold fast until the time we meet Jesus – when our sanctification and glorification will be complete).

This process of spiritual transformation, as I have already stated, begins at new birth. The first use of the term 'born anew'(or born again or from above) in the New Testament referring to new birth occurs in Jesus' fascinating discourse with Nicodemus, as recorded in John's Gospel chapter three. Seemingly ignoring Nicodemus' comments relating to Jesus' teaching credentials, Jesus answers:

"Truly, truly, I say to you, unless one is born anew, he cannot see the kingdom of God" (John's Gospel 3:3).

To Nicodemus, Jesus' words were alien to his thinking – he questions Jesus as to how a man can re-enter his mother's womb in order to be born physically a second time! But it is no coincidence that Jesus uses the illustration of new birth to describe the entry point into God's kingdom. When tied together with other New Testament scriptures, it is clear that Jesus was describing the beginning of a process of spiritual transformation which would last the whole of our lives. In fact, we need to see the parallel here between natural birth and growth into adulthood with spiritual new birth and transformation into spiritual maturity. Just as it would be impossible for a baby to remain as such without growth and development, the same is true spiritually – it should be impossible for a new-born believer to remain the same if the end goal is a transformation that prepares us to meet and to be like Jesus.

Glenys and I are proud parents of three wonderful children, who are now all grown up and married. We also have four wonderful grandsons. I would like you to imagine the scenario when our first child, Sarah, was born – family and friends flocking to see the new-born baby beautifully attired in white birth shawl. Imagine one month later, family and friends again come to see Sarah, but there has been no physical change whatsoever. What about six months later, one year later, five years later and still no change whatsoever! When I use this illustration in Africa, everyone bursts out into fits of laughter because the scenario described is impossible and ridiculous. The truth is that any baby that fails to grow and develop normally will usually die early and will certainly not reach its potential of maturity andadulthood. The same is true of spiritual birth – failure to grow spiritually and failure to be transformed, will lead to a failure to be transformed into the likeness of Jesus, and a failure to be ready to meet Him on His return.

Several times in the New Testament this process of spiritual transformation is described using terms such as 'babies', 'milk', 'young children', 'young men', 'solid food', 'mature', 'adults', 'fathers', etc. In his first letter to the Corinthian church, Paul addresses some of the believers there as being still "babes in Christ" rather than "spiritual men" because they were still "of the flesh", meaning that jealousy, strife and division were evident in their behaviour towards each other keeping them spiritually stunted (1 Corinthians 3:1-4).In Romans 8:12-13 Paul makes it clear that to continue to evidence the old 'flesh' life will lead to spiritual death rather than to eternal life. Jesus' parable of the sower (Matthew 13:18-23) carries the same implications – a farmer always sows seed with the expectation that it will result in a bountiful harvest, but there will always be some seed that germinates but, because of the soil it is planted in, it will eventually wither and die. Jesus likens the seed sown on rocky ground to the person who receives the gospel with joy but who only endures (continues in faith) for a while due to the onset of trouble or persecution.

The writer to the Hebrews rebukes those believers who ought to have matured to the point of being teachers of God's Word, but instead they still needed "milk, not solid food" and were still children in their spiritual understanding and levels of spiritual transformation (Hebrews 5:11-14).

In his letter to the Ephesian believers, Paul describes the purpose of the five-fold ministry gifts that Jesus has bestowed upon the Church – working together, their purpose is to unite and equip believers for ministry and to bring them to a place of mature manhood – to the place where they can actually measure themselves up against Jesus Himself. He adds that, to remain as spiritual children, exposes believers to destructive and harmful doctrinal error (implying that they could easily be drawn away from Christ), whereas, the need was to grow in maturity "into Christ" (Ephesians 4:11-16).

The problem in many churches is that the importance of taking new believers through to a place of spiritual maturity is not properly understood. Certainly, in Africa, where I have much experience of local church life, many pastors and leaders are content with seeing their churches filled with people, confessing that they are 'saved', but having no understanding of what it means to grow to maturity in Christ. Good, consistent Bible teaching is rare – what is mostly on the church agenda, week after week, is simple and often loud gospel preaching. The preaching may be stirring, and even exciting in its delivery but it rarely takes the believers far beyond the point of new birth. It has been said that the Church is Africa is a mile wide (referring to the numbers of people who attend churches across the Continent and the ease with which people appear to make an initial commitment to Christ) but only an inch deep (meaning that most believers remain as spiritual babies with little or no understanding of the need to grow into the likeness of Jesus). It's as if numbers and outward appearance in churches is held much higher than preparing believers to be like Jesus. But is the situation so different in other parts of the World? In the West there is certainly much more emphasis on Bible teaching in the churches, with a plethora of books, DVDs, and internet resources available, but I am not convinced that most believers really understand the 'Why?' and 'How?' of sanctification, leaving areas of their lives relatively untouched by the power of the gospel. Many are locked into a traditional evangelical understanding of the gospel which centres almost entirely on the new birth experience, an experience of the Holy Spirit (especially for the Pentecostals and Charismatics) and the future hope of eternal life in heaven. The part of spiritual life between new birth / experience of the Holy Spirit and the future hope of eternal life in heaven is largely not understood, apart from it being a time to win others for Christ and to continue in the practices expected of believers in Christ.

In his letter to the Colossian church, Paul describes what I would term the goal of all Christian ministry, where he writes:

"Him (Jesus) we proclaim, warning every man and teaching every man in all wisdom, that we might present every man mature in Christ" (Colossians 1:28).

Notice that Paul uses the word 'we'. Of course he would have been referring to the team that he was travelling with and also his fellow apostles, but, he was also reaching out to all of us across the generations – this is also *our* commission. For pastors, elders, teachers, evangelists, youth leaders, women's leaders, intercessors – the goal for each of us is not just to see people come to faith in Christ and to have a testimony that they are 'saved' but rather that each one is helped along in the process of spiritual transformation until they reach the goal of maturity in Christ. The help referred to consists firstly in proclaiming Jesus and all that he has achieved through his death and resurrection, then warning every person – both unbelievers and believers – to turn away and to continue to turn away from all iniquity and sin, and finally, to teach all believers with the end purpose of bringing them to maturity in Christ. What was this teaching to consist of? Well, Paul's words tie in perfectly with Jesus' words in the great commission, where the disciples were instructed to teach new believers to observe (Greek: 'terein' which carries the meaning of practically implementing and keeping strictly to) all that Jesus had taught and commanded them. In Colossians 1:29, Paul goes on to describe the total energy and effort, given and inspired by the Spirit, that he puts into this single-focused aim of presenting believers mature in Christ. This clearly suggests that the process of spiritual transformation is not one to be undertaken lightly or casually but rather one that is essential if we are to be conformed to the image of Jesus.

Our garden compound in Uganda is filled with all sorts of fruit trees and bushes, some of which were there when Glenys and I arrived in Kasese, and others which we planted, when we began to transform the compound from a weed-filled building site, full of stones, unused sand and cement into a delightful garden of lawns, flower beds and a fruit and vegetable area. Amongst the fruit growing in the garden were bananas (both sweet and matooke), passion fruits, mangoes, avocados, lemons, oranges, and tomatoes. In getting the point of Colossian 1:28 across to pastors and leaders being trained in our home, I would take a wicker basket and fill it with samples of various types of very immature fruit from the garden and then bring it along to class. At an appropriate point in the lesson I would offer the basket as a gift to one of the students. Of course, the response of the class was one of laughter with all agreeing that no-one, even with the most gracious of hearts, would really welcome such a gift – what really could be done with such a gift where the fruit would be totally unpalatable to eat. The point of the illustration is this: when we meet Jesus, what spiritual fruit will be offered to Him from the baskets of our lives and ministries? This applies firstly to us – the scriptural words 'transformed', 'maturity' and 'fruitfulness' really all refer to the same thing – being transformed into the likeness of Jesus. Will the process have been completed in us? What about the lives of those we have been ministering to – will they be unripe fruit or will they be at the point of being conformed to the image of God's Son as a result of our input into their lives?

You see, spiritual transformation is not an option in the life of a believer. There is no point in having a testimony of being 'saved' unless that testimony is matched by an ongoing process of spiritual transformation that is taking place in our lives up to the day we meet Jesus. Only this process will enable us to fulfil God's plan for us which is that we should resemble his Son.

In John's first letter, at one point, he addresses some comments to children, young men and fathers (1 John 2:12-14). Clearly, he is not literally writing to those in the church who, physically, were children, young men and fathers, but rather to believers who were in different stages of spiritual maturity. Each category of believer is addressed twice. To the 'children', John writes that their sins are forgiven and that they know the Father – these truths are primary spiritual truths learned early on in the lives of new believers. Sadly, though, large numbers have been believers for many years and yet they still have not grasped these fundamental truths. To the 'young men', John states twice that they are strong, and, in his second reference to them, he adds that the Word of God abides in them and that they have overcome the evil one – these references highlight the importance of the Word of God in bringing believers to a place of spiritual strength and maturity – it is only through reading and applying the Word of God in our lives that there is any hope of defeating the daily attacks of the evil one. Firstly, the 'milk' and then the 'meat' of the Word of God enable them to grow through to a place of spiritual adolescence. Notice how the young men referred to have overcome the evil one. When teaching on this passage in Africa, I would ask the question of the students, "How many of you would say you have reached the stage of spiritual young men?" The students referred to would often be pastors, overseers, even denominational Bishops, Bible School graduates and the like, but very few would testify that the evil one was really defeated in their lives. To the 'fathers', John writes that they know Him who is from the beginning. At first, I found this category of believers the hardest to explain. In the word, 'father' there is a sense of a real experience of knowing God deeply, a relationship which has probably been established over a number of years, but I felt that it must mean more as there are many believers, ofseveral years' standing, who sadly continue to be spiritual children – they know the spiritual routines and practices but lack true spiritual transformation in basic areas of their lives. I believe Paul gives a good understanding of what it means to be a spiritual father in his first letter to the Corinthians. He writes:

"For I became your father in Christ Jesus through the gospel. I urge you, then, be imitators of me" (1 Corinthians 4:15-16).

First and foremost, Paul is using the term 'father' in the sense of having been used by the Holy Spirit to give birth to spiritual children, referring the members of the Corinthian church. However, in what Paul writes, he also touches on the sort of lifestyle which should characterise a spiritual father – a lifestyle that can be imitated by others, and in doing so, will only bring them closer to Christ. A spiritual father, then, is one who is such an imitation of Jesus Himself that he can confidently encourage others to follow his example. How many pastors, leaders, youth leaders, and women's workers today could confidently stand up in front of their congregations and groups and encourage folk to imitate them spiritually, and in so doing, would expect their hearers to become more like Jesus – not just imitating their behaviour in a 'church' context, but imitating their attitudes, speech and behaviour behind closed doors in the home, within a marriage relationship, within the workplace, at school or college. If God's eternal plan is to see us conformed to the image of His Son, then aiming for spiritual fatherhood is a must – to be living examples today of the life and character of Jesus is an indicator that God's plan is truly being fulfilled in our lives.

The 'Why' of Sanctification

If Christ has paid the full price for our sin and we have been declared righteous in the sight of God (justification), then why do we need to be sanctified? This is a very important question, the answer of which we all need to fully understand.

Firstly, we need to define 'sanctification' – it is the process of being made holy, or set apart for holy use. There almost seems to be a contradiction here – we have been made holy in God's sight by the cleansing received through the blood of Jesus and yet we still need to be made holy! It might be helpful here to see holiness as both a gift and a walk – at the point of spiritual new birth we receive the gift of holiness, not by works but through placing our faith firmly in Christ and His work on the cross (Ephesians 2:8), but we then need to walk out this holiness through a transformed lifestyle with an end goal of being conformed to the image of the Lord Jesus Christ.

Although Christ has cleansed us from our sin, there is still a problem that needs to be dealt with in our lives that will keep us from becoming like Jesus – that problem is the presence of iniquity in our fallen human nature. Iniquity is that inner lawlessness and rebellion against God that manifests itself in a multitude of sinful motives, attitudes, words and actions, and which has been a part of mankind from the time that iniquity first entered the heart of Adam. Iniquity, if left unchallenged in our lives, even our 'saved' lives, will keep us from growing to spiritual maturity and into the likeness of Christ, unprepared to meet Him.

I want to clearly show you that this is a serious problem still for believers in Christ (although I am sure that we all recognise the outworking of iniquity within us!). One very important point, as we look into what God's Word says about this, is to remember that the New Testament letters were all written to believers within local churches founded by the various apostles. When issues of sinful practices are addressed the exhortations and warnings are not to unbelievers but to those who already have a relationship with God through His Son, Jesus. Listen then to some of the exhortations to these believers:

"Put off your old nature which belongs to your former manner of life and is corrupt through deceitful lusts" (Ephesians 4:22).

"Let us cast off the works of darkness and put on the armour of light; let us conduct ourselves becomingly as in the day, not in revelling and drunkenness, not in debauchery and licentiousness, not in quarrelling and jealousy" Romans 13:12-13),

"Put to death therefore what is earthly in you: fornication, impurity, passion, evil desire, and covetousness, which is idolatry …. But now put them all away: anger, wrath, malice, slander, and foul talk from your mouth" (Colossians 3:5-8).

All these manifestations of iniquity were obviously evident in the lives of those first believers. Does this mean that they were not truly 'saved'? Of course not- rather, it means that these people, who had entered the Kingdom of God throughspiritual new birth, who had the glorious seed of God implanted into their hearts, were now 'in process', 'being saved', needing to deal with the sinful attitudes, motives, words and actions that were still manifesting themselves as a result of their fallen human nature.

On several occasions, Paul reminds his readers that they have crucified the flesh (the old life with its sinful habits and practices),and that the old life had died and been buried with Christ. Baptism in water is a picture of this death that has taken place. In Romans chapter 6, where Paul uses the illustration of baptism as demonstrating death to the old life and resurrection to a new life in Christ, he writes:

"We know that our old self was crucified with Him so that the sinful body might be destroyed, and we might no longer be enslaved to sin" (Romans 6:6).

In his letter to the Galatian church, having just contrasted the works of the flesh with the fruit of the Spirit, Paul goes on to add:

"And those who belong to Christ Jesus have crucified the flesh with its passions and desires" (Galatians 5:24).

However, there are also several scriptures, including those already quoted earlier in this chapter, where Paul exhorts the believers – to 'put off', to 'cast off', to 'put to death' sin in their lives, implying that, the work of sanctification is both a past event but also a present and future action in our lives. This is clearly born out in scripture. For example, in 1 Corinthians 6:11, having just described the former unregenerate lives of believers, Paul writes:

"And such were some of you, but you were washed, you *were sanctified*, you were justified in the name of the Lord Jesus Christ and in the Spirit of our God".

However, in 1 Thessalonians 5:23, Paul writes:
"May the God of peace Himself *sanctify* you wholly."
Put simply: we have been made holy (sanctified) but there is still a work to be done in our lives in order that, day by day, we can walk in holiness (be sanctified), becoming more and more like Jesus.

So whose responsibility is it to deal with the iniquity in our lives? Is this work of sanctification an automatic action of the Holy Spirit in our lives now that we are children of God? Or is it all down to us to get our lives in order? The answer is 'a partnership' – sanctification is both a work of the Spirit but also involves action that we, ourselves, need to take. The amazing thing is, that even in the action we need to take, the Holy Spirit is the one who first convicts us of our sin, and then he is the one who strengthens and helps us to take the appropriate action – so, sanctification involves the activity of the Holy Spirit from beginning to end.

I personally believe that the work of sanctification in our lives is directly proportionate to the producing of God's glory within us, that we can only be "changed from one degree of glory to another" as we are putting to death the old life on a day by day basis. Iniquity and its outworking in various sinful habits and practices is a serious inhibitor to God's glory – even like a pathogenic virus, which, if it goes unchecked, will destroy the healthy life of living cells. If we choose to ignore iniquity in our lives, then there must be the possibility that our new life in Christ will be harmed and even destroyed, that any hope of being transformed into the likeness of Jesus will be taken from us.

Conformed to the Image of God's Son

The writer to the Hebrews uses the following very strong warning, as he addresses believers who were in danger of turning their backs on Christ and reverting to their old lives:
"Take care, brethren, lest there be in any of you an evil, unbelieving heart, leading you to fall away from the Living God, But exhort one another every day, as long as it is called "today", that none of you may be hardened by the deceitfulness of sin. For we share in Christ, if only we hold our first confidence form to the end" (Hebrews 3:12-14).
The Greek word '*ponera*', here translated as 'evil' can also mean malignant or slothful. In medical circumstances, to be tardy in dealing with a malignant tumour can have dire consequences – this is the seriousness of what is being expressed here: iniquity, if left unchecked and undealt with in the lives of believers can also have that dire consequence of leading us away from the life of God. The Greek word '*apaté*', here translated as 'deceitfulness' can also mean seduction. Such is the power of iniquity that we can easily be deceived and even be seduced by it, ignoring the need to deal with its deep roots in our lives.

In our compound in Uganda, the combination of hot sun and plentiful rain for most of the year led to a rapid growth of weeds, leaving our stony driveway quickly covered in unwanted vegetation in a matter of a few weeks. At first we would simply hoe the problem which was only ever a very short-term solution as the weeds quickly grew again. Before long we decided to use a systemic weed killer, where the active chemical is absorbed into the leaves of the weeds and absorbed right down to the roots, completely eradicating the problem. For many believers, the deceitfulness of sin, and our failure to grasp its serious consequences can often lead us to deal with the shoots at most, leaving the destructive roots of iniquity undealt with.

Here is something to think about – the blood of Jesus cannot and does not atone for unrepented iniquity and sin in the lives of believers. In other words, to confess that Jesus Christ has forgiven your sin at the point of new birth but to continue to ignore the ongoing presence of iniquity and its fruit – sin – in your lives will inevitably invite the judgment of God upon us. I don't believe that this will simply mean an exonerating slap on the wrist for us when we stand before the Lord, but rather the possibility of exclusion from His presence. Read what John writes, again remember it is to believers, in his first letter:

"Everyone who commits sin is guilty of lawlessness. You know that He appeared to take away sins, and in Him there is no sin. No one who abides in Him sins; no one who sins has either seen Him or known Him. Little children, let no one deceive you, He who does right is righteous, as He is righteous" (1 John 3:4-7).

When John speaks of committing sin he is speaking of the practice of sin as a continuous unrepented action rather than committing a sin from time to time – this is in keeping with the present continuous tense in the Greek language. We will all sin from time to time but there is forgiveness available in these circumstances (1 John 1:8-10), but a failure to deal with the *practice* of sin results in failing to continue to abide in and know Him. The ongoing practice of sin finds its root in 'lawlessness' (or rebellion - which is the definition of iniquity).

Conformed to the Image of God's Son

In Hebrews, the writer exhorts the believers to:
"Strive for peace with all men, and for the holiness without which no one will see the Lord. See to it that no one fail to obtain the grace of God" (Hebrews 12:14-15).

Here the writer is not talking about the gift of holiness given to us at the point of regeneration but rather a holiness (KJV uses 'sanctification' here) for which we need to strive (Greek *diokete* also translated as to eagerly follow after or acquire). Without this acquired holiness, which I would like to suggest is a life being increasingly stripped of the presence of iniquity and sin, no-one will even see the Lord; instead they will fail to be amongst the eternal recipients of God's grace.

In warning his readers about failing to obtain the grace of God, the writer to the Hebrews, exhorts them not to follow the example of Esau who easily gave up his legal birth-right in exchange for the fulfilment of his carnal appetite. Dealing with our 'fleshly' ungodly appetite is an ongoing struggle for all of us, not just Esau, but it is the only way to ensure a walk of holiness resulting in being able to meet God.

Thus ongoing sanctification in the life of a believer is not an option but rather it is an essential work: iniquity and its fruit – the practice of sin – cannot be ignored if we are going to fulfil God's call upon our lives to be conformed to the image of His Son.

Conformed to the Image of God's Son

the writer exhorts the believers to: ... of peace with all men, and for the holiness without which no one will see the Lord. See to it that no one fail to obtain the grace of God." (Hebrews 12:14-15).

Here the writer is ... talking about the gift of holiness given to us at the point of regeneration but rather a holiness (KJV uses 'sanctification' here) for which we need to strive (Greek 'diōkete,' also translated as to eagerly follow after or acquire). Without this acquired holiness, which I would like to suggest is a life being increasingly stripped of the presence of iniquity and sin, no one will even see the Lord; instead they will fail to be amongst the eternal recipients of God's grace.

In warning his readers about failing to obtain the grace of God, the writer to the Hebrews, exhorts them not to follow the example of Esau who easily gave up his legal birth-right in exchange for the fulfilment of his carnal appetite. Dealing with our 'fleshly, ungodly appetite' is an ongoing struggle for all of us, not just Esau, but it is the only way to ensure a walk of holiness resulting in being able to meet God.

Thus ongoing sanctification in the life of a believer is not an option but rather it is an essential work: iniquity and its fruit - the practice of sin - cannot be ignored if we are going to fulfil God's call upon our lives to be conformed to the image of His Son.

The 'How' of Sanctification

As stated in the last chapter the work of sanctification in our lives is a partnership between the Holy Spirit and ourselves – he transforms us day by day into the likeness of Jesus, changing us from one degree of glory to another but it is only in co-operation with us. We need to have a desire to be spiritually transformed and also be willing to take practical steps to change our ways – to deal with iniquity and sin in our lives that is offensive to God and which will prevent any transformation taking place. As also stated in the last chapter, even in the action we need to take, the Holy Spirit is the one who strengthens and helps us– therefore sanctification involves the activity of the Holy Spirit from beginning to end. So what practical steps do we need to take in order for the work of transformation to take place in our lives? These steps can be summed up as follows – Repentance, Renewing of the mind and Resistance.

Repentance is a key response in the life of a believer – it is foundational in the process of spiritual transformation. By definition, repentance is a total turnaround in our thinking which leads to a turnaround in our lives. Firstly, repentance is the doorway through which everyone needs to pass in order to enter the Kingdom of God. John the Baptist proclaimed "Repent for the kingdom of heaven is at hand" (Matthew 3:2); Jesus began his preaching ministry with "The time is fulfilled, and the kingdom of God is at hand; repent and believe in the gospel" (Mark 1:15); Peter, on the day of Pentecost answered the cry of his hearers by saying, "Repent, and be baptised everyone of you in the name of

Jesus Christ for the forgiveness of your sins; and you shall receive the gift of the Holy Spirit" (Acts 2:38). New life in Christ begins with repentance and faith – turning right away from our old life, receiving forgiveness for past sins, and placing our faith for new and eternal life in Jesus Christ.

However, repentance was never intended to be a one-off occurrence in our lives. As well as initially opening the door to forgiveness and new life in Christ, repentance is also the key to dealing with the problem of iniquity in our lives and to moving forward in the process of being transformed into the likeness of Jesus Christ.

Examples of the ongoing need for repentance in a believer's life can be found in Jesus' letters to the seven churches in Revelation chapters 2-3. It's interesting to note that the believers in five of those churches were called upon to repent. For those believers repentance was the key to being spiritual conquerors and to inheriting the rewards prepared for them in God's presence.

Paul, in his letters, only used the word 'repentance' or 'repenting' onthreeoccasions - addressing the Roman and Corinthian churches (2 Corinthians 7:9-10 and Romans 2:4) and to Timothy (2 Timothy 2:25); however, on a number of occasions he writes about repentance without actually using the word. In his letter to the Ephesian church he writes:
"Now this I affirm and testify in the Lord, that you must no longer live as the Gentiles …. *Put off* your old nature which belongs to your former manner of life and is corrupt through deceitful lusts" (Ephesians 4:17-22).

To the Roman believers he writes, in the context of the nearness of Jesus' return:

"Let us then *cast off* the works of darkness and put on the armour of light; let us conduct ourselves becomingly as in the day, not in revelling, not in debauchery and licentiousness, not in quarrelling and jealousy" (Romans 13:12-13).

Again to the Colossian church he writes:

"*Put to death* therefore what is earthly in you: fornication, impurity, passion, evil desire, and covetousness, which is idolatry. On account of these the wrath of God is coming. In these you once walked, when you lived in them, But now *put them all away*: anger, wrath, malice, slander, and foul talk from your mouths. Do not lie to one another, seeing that you have put off the old nature with its practices" (Colossians 3:5-9).

Paul, in these letters refers to repentance in terms of 'putting off', 'casting off', 'putting to death' and 'putting away'. In the example given from his letter to the Roman believers, Paul speaks of the soon coming of Jesus using the illustration of daylight fast approaching – just as there is a need to 'cast off' nightclothes and replace them with suitable clothing for the daytime, so it is with the sinful practices of the old life (born out of iniquity) – they all need to be 'cast off' in the light of preparing for Jesus' return. I have often used the example in Africa of a man returning from his shamba (field or garden) with dirty, sweaty clothes and soil-stained hands. What is the first thing he does? He completely strips off his old work clothes, then bathes, before putting on fresh, clean clothing. I have suggested that he might forego the washing and simply put the clean clothes directly over the dirty, smelly ones. Such a suggestion is always met with laughter. However, spiritually-speaking this is often what happens with believers who end up with a total mix of Christ-like virtues and fleshly practices. The Christ-like virtues are the ones we like to show off publicly, but, behind closed doors, it is often the fleshly practices that surface. The problem is that this is often seen as normal and the underlying iniquity and manifested sin is left undealt with.

Below, I have listed a number of steps which will help us to understand the process of repentance, of 'putting off' that needs to be taking place, almost certainly on a daily basis, in our lives:

- Firstly, as we read or listen to the Word of God we receive it by faith as God's word to us personally:
  "When you received the Word of God which you heard from us, you accepted it not as the word of men but as what it really is, the Word of God, which is at work in you believers" (1 Thessalonians 2:13).
  The primary way in which the Holy Spirit will get our attention is through the Word of God. If we read God's Word regularly and believe that He will speak to us through it, then He will use this as an opportunity to address areas of iniquity in our lives that need to be dealt with.

- We are convicted by the Holy Spirit as He takes the Word of God and applies it directly to our lives:
  "For our gospel came to you not only in word, but also in power and in the Holy Spirit and with full conviction" (1 Thessalonians 1:5).

It's amazing how, when we read God's Word with expectant faith, that a scripture will 'leap out' and hit us in our hearts, exposing areas that need to be dealt with (Hebrews 4:12-13) –we sense the Holy Spirit saying to us, as the prophet Nathan did to David, following his adultery, deception and complicity in murder, "You are the man" (2 Samuel 12:1-14). Be careful not to ignore the convicting voice of the Holy Spirit as it will inevitably lead to a hardening in your heart – you will learn to excuse your sinfulness. To reach such a point is almost a point of 'no return' and may bring you close to falling away from God (Hebrews 3:12-14).

- Understanding that God is holy, we confess our sins firstly to Him, recognising that the primary offence is against Him. We also confess our sins to those we have offended:
"For I know my transgressions, and my sin is ever before me. Against Thee, Thee only, have I sinned, and done that which is evil in Thy sight" (Psalm 51:3-4), and:
"Confess your sins to one another, and pray for one another" (James 5:16).
Although David sinned against a number of people following the episode of his adultery with Bathsheba, nevertheless, the primary offence was against God Himself. We will only truly understand such a position if a holy fear of God has been established in our hearts. At times, particularly if our sin is known to the one we have offended, there will also be the need to

confess our sin and to seek forgiveness of the one offended with sincerity and without excuse.

- We acknowledge our guilt before God with a godly sorrow:
  "For godly grief produces a repentance that leads to salvation"(Greek: 'lupé' – this literally means with grieving or brokenness as with the death of a loved one, 2 Corinthians 7:10).
  True repentance is not just saying 'sorry' (which often allows for a recurrence of the sinful activity). True repentance hits us hard like a grieving and with a brokenness for what we have thought, said or done.

- We seek forgiveness and ask God to change our heart by the power of His Spirit:
  "Create in me a clean heart, O God, and put a new and right spirit within me" (Psalm 51:10).
  We receive God's forgiveness and the cleansing of our hearts by faith.

- We put off our old nature by faith:
  "Put off your old nature which belongs to your former manner of life" (Ephesians 4:22).
  We need to understand that our old nature is no longer a part of who we are in Christ and so, by a statement of faith, we put if off. This will often involve a literal moving away from any possibility of a recurrence of the sinful activity – breaking unhelpful friendships and alliances, avoiding certain places and activities.

- We seek reconciliation with those we have offended, with a view to having restored relationships:
  "If one has a complaint against another, forgiving each other; as the Lord has forgiven you, so you also must forgive" (Colossians 3:13).
  Undoubtedly when we openly sin against others the result is broken relationships. True repentance includes seeking to restore those relationships to a place that honours God.

- We make restitution wherever possible. This means to restore to others that which has been taken from them – it might be money, goods, or their reputation and standing before other people. Zacchaeus, when he came to a place of true repentance, stated to Jesus:
  "Behold, Lord, the half of my goods I give to the poor; and if I have defrauded any one of anything, I restore it fourfold" (Luke 19:8).
  Engaging in sinful activity often has very real practical consequences. Experiencing God's forgiveness does not mean that we can simply ignore those from whom we have stolen, whether it be money, goods or their reputation. If your sin has involved gossiping against or slandering an individual in the sight of others, then all such conversations and comments will need to be properly rectified. This step means that 'saving face' is not an option for a truly repentant believer – one who seeks to save his own reputation and standing before others has never truly come to a place of repentance.

- We make ourselves accountable to godly leaders and fellow believers in order that they might stand with us in a new spiritual walk:
"Obey your leaders and submit to them; for they are keeping watch over your souls, as men who will have to give account. Let them do this joyfully, and not sadly, for that would be of no advantage to you" (Hebrews 13:17).
Sharing our weaknesses with godly leaders and friends will certainly help us to stand strong in times of temptation. Learn to give permission for others to speak into weak areas of your life. Again, don't seek to 'save face' in such areas.

- We make a firm choice not to re-visit the area of sin or to live in regret of the step of repentance we have taken:
"Forgodly grief produces a repentance that leads to salvation and brings no regret" (2 Corinthians 7:10).
The enemy of our souls, Satan, will regularly tempt us to think with regret on those things we have 'put away' – to rue things we have turned away from will inevitably lead to us re-engaging in those activities.

It's helpful, rather than to view repentance as a negative activity, to see the opportunity to repent as a precious gift from God, preventing you from falling away from Christ, and one which will enable you to advance in your spiritual transformation into the likeness of Jesus. Every area of iniquity and sin repented of creates space for the Holy Spirit to reproduce in you more of God's glory.

Renewing of the mind is moving to that place where we understand what Jesus Christ has done for us and who we now are in Christ – we have been cleansed by the blood of Jesus, we have been given new and eternal life, we have a new Father, we are already sons of the King of kings.

Often when teaching these wonderful truths in Africa, we casually ask the students, including pastors and leaders, in our training classes, "Who is your father?" The answers come back, "Nsangwa", ""Twesigomwe", "Kazora" – all referring to their natural lineage. We keep on asking the question until, at last, someone ventures to say, "God is my father", at which point we raise a loud "Hallelujah!" The whole point of the exercise is to demonstrate clearly, that although we have natural fathers, the greater truth is now we are children of a Heavenly Father.His eternal DNA runs through us and now determines our future. In the light of this, the thought patterns, attitudes, words, actions, habits and lifestyle, which belonged to the old order, are no longer ours to follow.Rather we allow the Holy Spirit to produce in us those qualities and characteristics that replicate those seen in Jesus and in our Heavenly Father.

In his second letter to the Corinthian church, Paul declares:
"From now on, therefore, we regard no one from a human point of view …. Therefore, if any one is in Christ, he is a new creation; the old has passed away, behold, the new has come" (2 Corinthians 5:16-17).
In Paul's mind it is as if he is saying that we are no longer 'homo sapiens', in reality dead through our trespasses and sins (Ephesians 2:1), but rather a new breed 'homo gloria',

made alive in Christ, recreated in the likeness of a glorious God. By faith we need to see ourselves in this light.

Paul states in his letter to the Ephesian believers:
"Now this I affirm and testify in the Lord, that we must no longer live as the Gentiles do …. put off your old nature which belongs to your former manner of life and is corrupt through deceitful lusts, and be renewed in the spirit of your minds, and put on the new nature, created after the likeness of God in true righteousness and holiness" (Ephesians 4:17,22-24).
By faith, we put on the new nature, knowing that God's seed is now implanted in our hearts, and, just as our Heavenly Father is righteous and holy, so it is now natural for us to evidence righteousness and holiness in our everyday lives.

In Mark Twain's fascinating novel, 'The Prince and the Pauper', identically-looking young men meet and decide to exchange positions in life for a season – one is a prince and the other is a pauper. Focusing on the pauper, when he entered the palace for the first time to take the place of the prince, he began a whole new episode in his life – he had to demonstrate that he was the prince which, for him (previously the pauper) was a major learning curve – he had to discard the pauper's clothes, behaviour and habits and adopt a whole new way of life, fitting of a prince. This involved a whole new way of thinking for him until he grew accustomed to his new lifestyle. For us as sons of the King of kings the same is true of us, except it is not only for a short season, as in Mark Twain's story, but for all eternity. The transformation into the lifestyle of a son of God begins here and now.

Reading on in Ephesians 4, from verse 25 to chapter 6 verse 9, Paul unpacks what it means to live as a son of God, "created after the likeness of God in true righteousness and holiness". He begins with a series of contrasts – instead of speaking lies (which belongs to the old nature), only speak the truth (evidence of the new nature); no longer steal (the old nature), but do honest work with your hands (the new nature) - notice how Paul adds here that the fruit of our honest labour will be that we can give to others in need – a total contrast from the habit of stealing which is unlawfully taking things from others; let no evil speech leave your mouths (the old nature), instead speak only that which edifies others (the new nature); put away bitterness, anger and slander (the old nature), instead be kind, compassionate and forgiving (the new nature); put away all types of impurity and filthy speech (the old nature), instead let your speech be filled with thanksgiving to God (the new nature); don't get drunk on wine (the old nature), but be filled with the joy that the Holy Spirit brings (the new nature). Paul then goes on to speak of how our new nature needs to permeate even our everyday relationships - between husbands and wives, between parents and children and between employers and employees.

In our training programmes in Africa perhaps the most challenging area addressed is how this new life in Christ needs to be evidenced in the home (I know that the same is true of the West). We now have many testimonies from husbands who have returned to their homes, after being trained, with renewed minds, repenting before their wives and children, willing to startafresh in their marriages and family life, seeing their wife no longer as an object of work to be possessed, but rather a treasured wife to be loved "as Christ loved the Church" (Ephesians 4:25).

In his letter to the Colossian church, having listed various manifestations of iniquity that need to be 'put to death' or 'put off' – anger, wrath, malice, slander, foul talk and lying – Paul then goes on to list those characteristics that need to be put on – compassion, kindness, lowliness, meekness, patience, forgiveness and love (Colossians 3:5-14). It's remarkable how similar these characteristics that need to be 'put on' are to the fruit of the Spirit in Paul's letter to the Galatians (Galatians 5:22-23):
"But the fruit of the Spirit is love, joy, peace, patience, kindness, goodness, faithfulness, gentleness, self-control". This fruit is, in essence, a summary of the character of Jesus Himself. By faith, and in practice, and with the help of the Holy Spirit, we put on these godly characteristics. The Holy Spirit then takes our renewed thoughts, attitudes, words and actions and from them produces lasting fruit. In other words, we are beginning to "put on the Lord Jesus Christ" (Romans 13:14).

Resistancemay well be the hardest of these three steps to spiritual transformation in the ongoing process of sanctification. If there's one thing that the Devil hates it is a believer who is taking serious steps to be transformed into the likeness of God's Son. If you are content with a testimony of being 'saved' but in reality that confession is having little visible effect in your life then there's little he needs to do – your self-deception is doing it all for him! The Devil hates Jesus and he hates God's plans and purposes for mankind. He also knows that his time is short and he is determined to take down as many as possible when he is banished to Hell.

When a person is truly born anew, God's seed is planted into his or her heart. Using a different illustration, it is like a bridgehead being established in a person's life well within enemy territory. God's plan for you is to gradually retake the territory of your heart, pushing the enemy back and out. As long as iniquity remains firmly rooted in your life, then the enemy has a strong foothold and it is impossible for you to be transformed into Jesus' likeness. I have a son who is good at rock climbing – I remember watching him some years back, scaling a rock face in Derbyshire, England. I was amazed at the smallness of the cracks and ledges that he needed to gradually work his way upwards. It's the same with the Devil. He requires the smallest of opportunities to establish a foothold in our lives. Therefore Paul exhorted the Ephesian believers:
"Give no opportunity to the devil" (Ephesians 4:27 – in the NIV 'opportunity' is translated as 'foothold'). We need, through repentance, to make smooth every possible foothold in our lives and then to make sure that no further cracks appear.

I recall, at one time, hearing teaching about our spiritual enemy, the Devil, from Peter's first letter (1 Peter 5:8-9) – stating that the Devil is like a roaring lion, but roaring is all

he can do, because he is a toothless lion! Don't you believe it
- I have seen many true believers fall by the wayside over the
years because they failed to ignore the warning signs, failed
to deal with iniquity that had established a strong root in
their lives, believers who lived with regrets and
disappointments that opened wide the door to the Devil.
Where are those believers today? A long way from the
Kingdom of God - a million miles away from being conformed
to the image of God's Son, and therefore totally unprepared
to meet the Lord. Skeletons (undealt with iniquity) left in the
cupboards of our hearts have an embarrassing and destructive
habit of reappearing when the Devil knows they will do the
most damage!

In his letter to the Ephesians, Paul exhorts the believers to:
"Be strong in the Lord and in the strength of His might. Put
on the whole armour of God,that you may be able to stand
against the wiles of the devil .... Therefore take the whole
armour of God, that you may be able to withstand in the evil
day, and having done all, to stand" (Ephesians 6:10-13).
The way to resist the Devil is to make sure that we are
continually clothed in God's armour. But what does this
entail? I remember hearing a Christian brother state, as a
spiritual exercise, that every morning he ensures he is
clothed in each piece of spiritual armour. I have to admit to
thinking rather naughtily, "What happens to the armour
during the night"! It's important to realise, when you read
about the different pieces of armour referred to in chapter
six, that all of them are rooted firmly in the Word of God -
loins girded with truth - truth that comes from the Word of
God; the breastplate of righteousness - the understanding of

which comes from the Word of God; feet shod with the equipment of the gospel of peace – a gospel which is found within the Word of God, and so on. It's not so important to daily recite and make declarations about the different pieces of spiritual armour as it is to make sure that the Word of God is being obeyed and lived out each and every day – then the spiritual protection will be complete, each piece of the armour will remain in place. As John stated regarding spiritual 'young men', the key to their defeating of the Evil One was a strength discovered through applying the Word of God to their lives.

When Jesus addressed the seven churches in Revelation chapters two and three, he exhorted all of them to be spiritual conquerors. It is important to note that it is only spiritual conquerors who are promised the reward, firstly, of making it into God's presence and who are then promised rewards when in God's presence. Let me explain: these rewards include the right to eat eternally from the tree of life (chapter 2:7), protection from the second death (chapter 2:11), having names that will not be removed from the book of life (chapter 3:5) – these three rewards are guarantees that overcoming believers will inherit eternal life with Christ. For the reward mentioned in chapter 3 verse 5 to mean anything, it must imply that failing to be a conqueror will result in the removing of a believer's name from the book of Life! Other rewards for conquerors mentioned in these seven letters include: the receiving of a new name, previously known only to God, written on a white stone (chapter 2:17), the right to share in ruling over the nations (chapter 2:26); the right to be a pillar within God's Temple (chapter 3:12), and the right to rule alongside Jesus on His throne (chapter 3:21).

This may sound obvious but a conqueror is someone who has had to conquer something. In British history, William the Conqueror, the Norman invader, gained his name through conquering and subjecting the territory of Britain to his rule. The major battle in which we have to be conquerors, as believers, is the battle that is taking place within our own souls, the battle against iniquity – seeing it uprooted and removed once and for all time from our lives. Often this is a fierce battle, because we are advancing on long-held ground of the enemy. However, the good news is that we have been given both the spiritual weapons and the powerful assistance of the Holy Spirit to enable us to overcome in this battle. The victorious position that we are able to maintain, if we walk in obedience to the Holy Spirit, is that of being "more than conquerors through Him who loved us" (Romans 8:37).

The three steps of repentance, renewing of the mind and resistance, are therefore key to spiritual transformation and to us being conformed to the image of God's Son, the Lord Jesus. As you will understand, these three steps are not one-off steps but they will need to be taken each and every day of our lives until the time we meet Jesus. However, every time we take these three steps we move forward, we are further transformed, more of God's glory is fashioned within us. Let's continue to move forward until God's wonderful plan for our lives is fulfilled. As Jesus stated in Matthew's gospel:
"He who endures to the end will be saved" (Matthew 24:13).

Prepared for the Soon Coming of Jesus

The prophetic scripturesin God's Word are all indicating that the return of Jesus will be happening very soon, even in our generation. In Matthew chapter 24, we have a lengthy teaching, where Jesus, in response to the disciples' question concerning the future destruction of the Temple in Jerusalem and the sign of His coming, outlines a number of prophetic signs that will precede His return. Tying this passage in with corresponding passages in Mark chapter 13 and Luke chapter 21, we quickly come to the conclusion that His return is indeed near. Let me outline just a few signs from those chapters, ones which either have been or are being fulfilled in this generation.

It is no coincidence that Jesus used the term "birth-pangs" relating to a number of signs that will sound the alarm for his imminent return – He spoke of false Christs appearing (Greek: 'christōs' can also be translated 'anointed ones' which I believe is a more helpful translation here), nations (Greek: 'ethnōs' can also be translated as 'tribes') rising up against each other, famines and earthquakes. Of course all these signs have been happening since the time of Christ so what is so significant here? To give one example - in the last fifty years there has been an amazing increase in natural disastersaround the world, which, when plotted on a graph reach a point ofalmost exponential increase. In fact, such a graph could easily be mistaken for one hanging at the foot of a hospital bed, a graph which might be used to monitor the increase in frequency and intensity of birth pains for a woman in the final stages of labour. Such a graph would clearly indicate the imminent birth of a baby. I believe that Jesus was pointing out something similar with regard to the "birth-pangs" signs – when these signs are taking place in an exponential way then His return is imminent. In the nations surrounding our home in Western Uganda, there are numerous rebel, tribal and regional conflicts taking place right now – no sooner does one cease then another one commences. In the African Church today many false leaders are rising up stating that they are the 'anointed ones' (Is the West so different?). These are clear indicators that Jesus' return is imminent.

Perhaps the most significant sign in our generation has been the restoration of Israel as a sovereign nation after almost 2000 years without a homeland. In 1948, against all the odds, Israel again became an independent nation, and, also, against all the odds of survival, has maintained its status even though surrounded by vastly bigger hostile nations intent on its destruction. In 1967, at the end of the 'Six Day' war, Israel recaptured the whole of Jerusalem, which once again became the capital of Israel – the first time since its destruction by the Roman army is AD70. In Luke chapter 21, Jesus prophesied that Jerusalem would be downtrodden by all nations, with the Jews scattered and led captive all over the world, until the "times of the gentiles" are fulfilled (Luke 21:23-24). Paul, in his letter to the Roman church, also refers to the times of the gentiles – he writes referring to the time in history when God's purposes for the gentile nations will be complete, which will then be followed by a major turning to God by the Jewish people. The context for Paul's comments is clearly an end-times scenario:

"Lest you be wise in your own conceits, I want you to understand this mystery, brethren: a hardening has come upon part of Israel, until the full number of the Gentiles has come in, and so all Israel will be saved" (Romans 11:25-26).

In these lastfew decades, since the re-capture of Jerusalem, there has been a remarkable influx of Jews into Israel from numerous nations around the world, making 'aliyah' (Hebrew for 'ascent' or 'the act of going up') to Israel and fulfilling several Old Testament Messianicscriptures pointing to this time. Jeremiah contains one such end-times prophesy:

"Therefore, behold, the days are coming, says the Lord, when men shall no longer say, 'As the Lord lives who brought up the people of Israel out of the land of Egypt', but 'As the Lord lives who brought up and led the descendants of the house of Israel out of the north country and out of all the countries where He had driven them'. Then they shall dwell in their own land" (Jeremiah 23:7-8).

For many years now, that tiny nation of Israel has been the focus of world news, and clearly the pieces are being put into place for that final 'show-down' centring on Israel and on Jerusalem that will usher in Jesus' return as King of kings and Lord of lords.

Space doesn't permit me to go into greater detail here concerning the prophetic signs preceding Jesus' return, and that is not the purpose of this book, rather just to say that Jesus is surely coming soon and all believers need to be ready for that great event.

A Church of Uganda minister used to teach his congregation about the need to be ready for the soon coming of Jesus.

"Are you ready?" he would regularly ask his church members, to which they would always reply, "Yes, we are ready". One day he decided to challenge his hearers in a different way – he clothed his curate in a long white gown and asked him to climb into the roof area of the church and await his call. The challenge went out again that day to the congregation, "Are you ready for Jesus' coming?" Again the response was as normal "Yes, we are ready". "Are you sure you are ready?" asked the minister. "Yes, we are sure" was the reply. The minister continued, "Things are so difficult for us, there are so many challenges – sickness, poverty, hunger, corruption – why don't we ask Jesus to come back now and take us home with him? Shall we ask him to come back now? Are you ready for Him?" In unison, the congregation replied, "Yes, we are ready". At that point, the minister paused and then prayed, crying out, "Jesus we know you are returning soon, but you know the challenges that we are facing – sickness, poverty, hunger, corruption. Will you not come back even now? Deliver us from our challenges, take us home to be with you forever". Immediately a section of the ceiling parted and the curate appeared clothed in his white gown. With his arms outstretched he shouted in a very loud voice, "Pah!" (An African expression used to surprise others). As one man, the congregation leapt to their feet and ran out of the church as fast as they could, screaming, "Jesus has come back, Jesus has come back – we are not ready, we are not ready!" Some, who ran ahead of the others, reached a local bar, where the customers were downing beers. "Jesus has come back, Jesus has come back!" the church members shouted. "Where is he?" the bar customers replied. "He is in the church" was the response. Immediately the bar customers threw down their beers and fled the bar, shouting "Jesus has come back and we are drinking beer – he mustn't find us here, we are not ready, we are not ready!"

This is a highly amusing story but it also has a very clear message: many believers would state their readiness for Jesus' return, as did these Church of Uganda members, but the truth is they are not. Often I have challenged congregations in Africa with the same question "Are you ready for the soon coming of Jesus?" (but without the curate to back up my question!). The reply is always "Yes, we are ready". However, the opposite is quickly seen to be the case when the congregation are challenged about how they live together as husbands and wives, how they treat their children, how they handle their finances, the things they are holding in their hearts – unforgiveness, bitterness, hatred, jealousy, lying, etc.

Paul, in his first letter to the Thessalonian church, writes about the first event that will happen when Jesus returns – the rapture of all true believers from every generation. His teaching came about as a result of a situation in the Thessalonian church, where, in the context of a strong belief in the early Church that Jesus' return was imminent, some believers had, meanwhile, died. Did this mean that they would miss out on God's plans and purposes for them? Paul assures the believers that both those who had died and those who are still alive at Christ's coming will rise to meet Him in the air (1 Thessalonians 4:13-18). The truth is that believers in every generation have needed to be prepared for Jesus' return. This rapture will be the next thing that happens for all those who have died "in Christ" - they will meet Jesus in the air and then experience the final transformation into His likeness. Being "in Christ" is a key theme in Paul's letters, where he is writing about the position of all true believers, who know Jesus Christ as their Saviour and Lord. Being "in Christ" is the qualification referred to in the Thessalonian letter ensuring readiness for Christ's return. The writer to the Hebrews also uses a very similar term to "in Christ" when he challenges his readers that "sharing in Christ" (and his salvation) is only a certainty for those who hold their "first confidence firm to the end" (Hebrews 3:14). The context for this statement, as we have already stated in a previous chapter, is one of the possibility of believers falling away from the Living God as a result of failing to deal with the presence of iniquity and sin in their lives. Therefore to ensure that we remain "in Christ" and therefore are ready to meet Jesus we need to continue in that ongoing process of spiritual transformation.

Paul illustrates this truth vividly in his first letter to the Corinthian believers, where, using the example of an athlete in training who is running for the victor's crown, he writes that he disciplines (Greek: 'hupopiazo' which can be translated as 'strike in the face' or 'beat black and blue') his body spiritually "lest after preaching to others I myself should be disqualified" (1 Corinthians 9:24-27). It's almost unthinkable to consider Paul as being unprepared for the return of Jesus but these are his very words. Paul wasn't speaking about rigorous and self-harming spiritual disciplines here (as practised at different times throughout Church history), but rather a recognition that there was still a fierce battle to engage in, one of defeating iniquity which resides in the fallen human nature. In fact Paul's words are supported by what he writes in his letter to the Philippian church. Paul had spoken of the surpassing worth of knowing Christ, and receiving His righteousness through faith – his goal was now to attain the resurrection from the dead (at the return of Christ) – he writes:

"Not that I have already attained this or am already perfect; but I press on to make it my own, because Christ Jesus has made me His own. Brethren, I do not consider that I have made it my own; but one thing I do, forgetting what lies behind and straining forward to what lies ahead, I press on toward the goal for the prize of the upward call of God in Christ Jesus" (Philippians 3:12-14).

For Paul, the prize he was aiming for was to be a part of the rapture (the upward call of God – this Greek used in this phrase has a sense of literally being called upwards) but he recognised that there was still further perfecting or spiritual maturing to ensure he reached his goal. You see, it's possible, even for those who are engaged in preaching and teaching the Word of God, to end up disqualified from receiving the reward of eternal life and transformation into the likeness of Jesus due to a failure to continue in the process of spiritual transformation following new birth in Christ.

John, in his first letter, also refers to the return of Jesus and the transformation that is due to be completed in the lives of all true believers at that time:

"Beloved, we are God's children now; it does not yet appear what we shall be, but we know that when He appears we shall be like Him, for we shall see Him as He is" (1 John 3:2).
He then goes on to make the very poignant comment:
"And every one who thus hopes in Him purifies himself as he is pure" (verse 3).
It is one thing to believe in Jesus' soon coming but that belief demands personal preparation – it is the responsibility of all true believers to make sure that their lives are pure and the measure of that purity is the character of Jesus Himself.

Paul, when writing to the Ephesian church, compares the relationship between a husband and wife to that between Christ and the Church. He writes that Christ's overriding purpose is to present the Church to Himself as holy and without blemish, a sanctified Bride, whose deep cleansing will come about as a result of being washed thoroughly with the Word of God (Ephesians 5:25-27) – this cleansing takes place when there is a daily obedient response to the Holy Spirit as He takes the Word of God and applies it directly to our lives.

John, towards the end of the book of Revelation, presents 'the other side of the coin' to what Paul writes concerning the Bridegroom's intentions – he reveals that the Bride also has to take personal responsibility in this preparation for Christ's return:
"Let us rejoice and exult and give Him the glory, for the marriage of the Lamb has come, and His Bride has made herself ready" (Revelation 19:7).

The readiness of the Bride, in this passage, is due to her "righteous deeds" (verse 8), which can only ever be birthed out of a righteousand transformed heart.

Peter, in his second letter, writes, partly, to deal with the issue of scoffers who were questioning the return of Jesus – they had been saying:
"Where is the promise of His coming? For ever since the fathers fell asleep, all things have continued as they were from the beginning of creation" (2 Peter 3:4).
The scoffers themselves are not identified in the letter – perhaps they were enemies of the gospel or perhaps they were believers who had become disillusioned with the delay in Jesus' coming.
Peter, in answering these scoffers, writes of the judgment that God brought about in the days of Noah through a worldwide flood which wiped out sinful mankind – in other words things had not remained the same since the time of creation. Just as God judged the world then, so a time would soon come when God would again judge the world. Following this warning, Peter exhorts the believers to live holy and godly lives as they eagerly await the coming day of God. True believers are encouraged to be zealous (Greek: 'spoudasate' can also be translated 'to be bent upon, to strive, to be earnest') to be found on that day "without spot or blemish, and at peace" (2 Peter 3:11-14). So, again, there is the call for holiness and purity. I believe that the peace being spoken about by Peter is one of knowing that all iniquity revealed by the Holy Spirit in the lives of those believers had been dealt with thoroughly, leaving an assurance of readiness for Christ's return.

A scripture referred to in an earlier chapter states that without a striving after holiness "no-one will see the Lord" (Hebrews 12:14) and therefore demands the response from believers of earnestly seeking to live holy lives. As stated earlier, this is referring to a walk of holiness that must be the outworking of the gift of holiness received through faith in Jesus Christ.

But isn't there a danger here of promoting a type of salvation by works? Isn't there a suggestion that what Christ achieved through His death on the cross is not enough? Where is the assurance of our salvation with such teaching?

Without question, our salvation is firmly grounded in the finished work of Jesus Christ upon the cross. Jesus paid the full price for our sins and also turned away the wrath of God from all of us, who fully deserved it. This salvation, as we have stated, is personally appropriated when we turn to God in true repentance and faith and, in return, we receive his forgiveness and new life through Jesus Christ. In the New Testament this is referred to as being born anew, born again or born from above (John 3:3; 1 Peter 1:23). At this point the seed of God enters our hearts. We are declared to be righteous in God's sight (justified). However, this is clearly only a beginning – it's absolutely true that no further sacrifice is needed for our sins, but there is a need for sanctification and glorification to take place within our lives. Justification without sanctification and glorification is impossible as the goal of our salvation is not just forgiveness of sins and new and eternal life, but it is full transformation into the likeness of Jesus Himself. This does not happen at new birth, which is just the beginning of the process, but rather it is a day by day change which needs to take place in our lives – one which happens through the partnership of both the Holy Spirit and ourselves. The Holy Spirit is always wanting to do a work within our lives but we also have a work to do – a willing submission to the will and plans of God for us, which includes an increasing walk of holiness and purity. So the assurance of our salvation is not based on a past event or experience, however real and transforming that event was. That event of new birth needs to take place in all of our lives, but our assurance is based on a continuing walk with God and a continuing spiritual transformation taking place. Today I need to be right with God, today I need to listening to the Holy Spirit, today I need to be turning away from all revealed iniquity and sin, today I need to be longing to be like Jesus, today I need to be eagerly looking forward to His return – then today I will be ready to meet Him and be fully transformed into His likeness.

All true believers in Jesus Christ, who know the reality of a 'today' salvation in their lives, will certainly be amongst that multitude who see Jesus' glorious face shining like the sun. At that very moment the spiritual transformation in their lives will be completed – they will be fully conformed to the image of God's Son - they too will radiate that same divine glory through their resurrected bodies for all eternity

The songwriter and worship leader, Matt Redman, writes in his song, 'Holy':
"And You shall come again in glory
To judge the living and the dead;

All eyes will look on Your glorious face,
Shining like the sun,
Who is like You, God?"

The sentiment of this wonderful song is that no-one compares to Jesus, and we shall understand that when one day we see Him as He truly is, in all His radiant glory. In the context of the song lyrics the words "Who is like you, God?" is intended to draw out the response, "Absolutely no-one!" Of course, Jesus is and has been, and always will be the unique and eternal all-glorious Son of God. However, an equally valid response on that day to the question "Who is like You, God?" would be "We are!" Remember John categorically states that "we shall be like Him, for we shall see Him as he is" (1 John 3:2).

In another of his worship songs, 'Endless Hallelujah', Matt Redman writes:
"When I stand before Your throne
Dressed in glory not my own
What a joy I'll sing of on that day
No more tears or broken dreams
Forgotten are the minor things
Everything as it was meant to be."

The glory we will be dressed in, on Jesus' return, will be a mirror image of His glory, as we will then be fully transformed "into His likeness" (2 Corinthians 3:18), experiencing that "eternal weight of glory beyond all comparison" (2 Corinthians 4:17). At that very moment God's eternal plan for our lives, the fullness of the 'good news' will be completed in our lives.

Hallellujah and hallelujah!